It's God's Business

Your Road to Success

Shannon Barnes

Copyright © 2015

Shannon Barnes

It's God's Business
Your Road to Success

Copyright © 2015 by Shannon Barnes
Baker, LA
All Rights Reserved

Scripture quotations, unless otherwise stated, are taken from the King James Version of the Holy Bible.
All Rights Reserved.

No portion of this book may be used, reproduced, or transmitted in any form or by any means, electronic or mechanical, including photocopying, recording, scanning, or any information storage and/or retrieval system, without permission in writing from the publisher.

Warranty Disclaimer/Limits of Liability

This publication is designed to provide information in regard to the subject matter covered. It is sold with the understanding that the publisher and author is not engaged in rendering physiological, financial, legal, or other licensed services. The publisher and author make no representations or warranties with respect to the completeness of the contents of this work. The publisher and author shall have neither liability nor responsibility to anyone with respect to any loss or damage caused, or alleged to be caused, directly or indirectly by the information contained in this book. The publisher and author make no representation that utilizing the strategies contained herein will automatically guarantee success. This book is strictly for informational and educational purposes.

Printed in the United States of America

ISBN-13: 978-0692477328
ISBN-10: 0692477322

Acknowledgments

First, all praise, honor and glory goes to my Lord and Savior, Jesus Christ, from Who all blessings flow. If it had not been for His grace, mercy and unmerited favor bestowed upon me, I don't know where I would be, nor would this book have become a reality.

Secondly, I would like to give heart-felt thanks with sincere gratitude to my husband and children for their unwavering support during this endeavor. Their daily prayers, patience, support and love have been extremely important to me during the writing of this book.

Next to my Mother, my Rock, my Counselor, my Walking Billboard, my Marketer, my Endorser, and my Advisor, who has always been there to encourage me in ALL my ideas and through all my many business ventures. I have the best Mother on this side of heaven. Love you, Pee!!

Next to my brother, my twin baby sisters, my sister-in-law, my nieces and my nephew, whose unconditional love and indescribable support have been an essential source of strength and encouragement throughout this process.

Additional acknowledgment goes to none other than my spiritual Father and First Lady whose prayers and support are invaluable. YOU ALREADY KNOW!!! Thank you for your guidance, your prayers, and your listening ear in ALL things!!!!

This book is truly a testament that with God, **all things are possible**.

DEDICATION

This book is dedicated to my older sister, Kimberley Grant, my buddy, my teaser, my "partner-in-crime". You departed this earth much too soon. I miss your hearty laugh, my "hipping you to the dial tone" (family insider), and the way we reminisced about our childhood in New Orleans. I know you are looking down and saying,
"You go, girl!!"
You will forever be in my heart.
I love and miss you so much.
My soul tells me you are proud!!

I LOVE YOU BUT GOD LOVED YOU MORE!!!

This book is written for every person either wanting to start, grow or expand a business, from" just a thought" phase to visual conception. It is my intent to show each entrepreneur that just as God's Word is the roadmap of daily living, so it is that same road map to entrepreneurs. This book is geared to give you important information that you wouldn't otherwise receive via conventional means or methods.

Table of Contents

Chapter 1	Introduction	....	07
Chapter 2	Mindset Change	....	26
Chapter 3	Is It Right For You?	....	35
Chapter 4	Prosperity Plan	....	47
Chapter 5	Fear Factor	....	56
Chapter 6	Make It Legal	....	62
Chapter 7	Branding	....	71
Chapter 8	Endurance	....	74
Chapter 9	Write the Vision	....	78
Chapter 10	Conclusion	....	82

1
INTRODUCTION

God's Holy Word is the blueprint for daily living, inclusive of marriage, children, loving one another unconditionally, forgiveness, and yes, even business ownership. I bet you never knew that God would have His own set of blueprints written exclusively for His people, even when it came to business ownership. Business ownership is one of the most exciting endeavors you will ever undertake. It is filled with uncertainties, but exploding with great joy and satisfaction.

It is IMPERATIVE that you understand that business success is just a TOUCH away. Through prayer, supplication and obedience, you are GUARANTEED SUCCESS. Just obey God's Word. It's just that simple.

> ### *Joshua 1:8*
> *. . . but thou shalt meditate . . day and night . . . for then thou shalt make thy way prosperous, and then thou shalt have good success.*

His Word instructs us to not only meditate on His Word, but that it should be done DAY AND NIGHT. This means that God's Word should be so embedded within our hearts and in our minds that we are ever constant of it in our daily lives. It is then AND ONLY THEN that we are ensured that our way will be made prosperous and that we shall have SUCCESS. To me there is nothing sweeter than to have God's assurance that He will make my way prosperous and give me success. If God says it, then it's SEALED, SIGNED, and DELIVERED.

Not only are we guaranteed SUCCESS, but we are guaranteed GOOD SUCCESS. Do we fully understand what a "guarantee" is? A guarantee is a promise that a certain thing will surely come to pass. A guarantee is the assurance that certain conditions will be met. You are ASSURED that God's Word cannot lie. You are ASSURED that God's Word cannot fail. You are ASSURED that God's Word will be fulfilled. Never forget that God has been, still is, and will continue to be in the blessing business.

Isn't it wonderful to know that your business won't open and then close without having seen the fruits of your labor? Isn't it wonderful to know that your business will earn its SUCCESS through integrity and not through manipulation? Isn't it wonderful to know that you have the Most High God as collateral? Isn't it wonderful to know that once God places His stamp of approval upon your business nothing can deter it from SUCCESS? That's enough to take a short praise break RIGHT NOW!!!

Once we have fully accepted Christ as our Lord and Savior, wanting to please Him becomes an everyday task. Once we have fully accepted Christ as our Lord and Savior, wanting to bask in His presence becomes an everyday occurrence. Once we have fully accepted Christ as our Lord and Savior, wanting to see Him again in His glory becomes an everyday desire.

For purposes of this book, a new definition of SUCCESS has been created:

Start Under Christian Character to Ensure Spiritual Satisfaction

We are certain to have SUCCESS in our lives as we build upon our Christian character. Building this character is a daily task which is sure to bring along with it many bumps and some occasional bruises. Being a Christian doesn't mean that we won't have our times of turmoil, disappointment and heartache. But, as Christians, we understand that it's all working together for our good. As Christians, we understand that the tumultuous times build us. As Christians, we understand that the disappointments help to make us fit for the Master's use. As Christians, we understand that even through the heartaches, God will never leave us nor will He ever forsake us. We know to get up, dust off our feet, and keep it moving.

As we build our Christian character, it will have no choice but to run over not only into our daily lives, but in that of our business ventures as well. This same Christian character will allow our businesses to flourish professionally, proficiently, LEGALLY, honestly, and filled with INTEGRITY. If we apply our Christian core values, we know that, in the end, we are VICTORIOUS.

As Christians (Believers) we are certain for SUCCESS in our everyday lives by following God's plan for our lives. It is His will for our lives and not our will that will ultimately sustain us.

Remember, your life is NOT your own. You belong to God. If we can just take a moment and meditate on the fact that we are God's!! If we can just take a moment and meditate on the fact that nothing is ours. Everything we have and everything we can ever hope to gain in the future comes from God and therefore belongs to Him and Him alone.

---
1 Corinthians 6:19
What? Know ye not that your body is the temple of the Holy Ghost which is in you, which ye have of God, and ye are not your own?

And because He owns EVERYTHING, how much then will He withhold from you??? YOU don't belong to you AND, your business doesn't belong to you. It's NOT yours. It belongs to the Lord.

Psalm 37:4
Delight thyself also in the Lord; and he shall give thee the desires of thine heart.

Keep this in mind. Never forget this fact. He says that we can have the desires of our heart. If it is your desire to have a business, then a business is what you shall have. Just make sure that you delight yourself in the Lord. Exactly what does it mean to delight oneself in something?

Well, to delight oneself in something simply means you find complete fulfillment and satisfaction in something. So, to delight yourself in the Lord simply means that God fulfills and satisfies everything in your life. In God there's peace. In God there's everlasting joy. In God there's comfort and serenity.

As Believers, it is imperative that we follow God's plan for our lives. If done so, it is a certain GURANTEE that you will have SUCCESS in whatsoever you place your hands to do, in Jesus' Name. Once we have acknowledged that plan, it is up to us to walk IN that plan. No detours. Going to the left is NOT an option. Going to the right is NOT an option. Not moving when He tells you to move is NOT an option. Delaying in moving is NOT an option. Move when God says move. Go where God says go. Do what God says do. Don't be disobedient. It's just that simple.

<u>1 Samuel 15:22</u>
... Behold, to obey is better than sacrifice,...

Remember Jonah? Jonah was given specific instructions from the Lord. But due to disobedience, Jonah had to be taken in a totally different direction. One thing I would like for everyone to take from Jonah's story is the simple fact that, in the end, you will have no choice but to obey God. You can "sike" yourself into believing that your way is the better way. Ultimately, it's God's way or NO WAY. You may kick and scream, but it will be done God's way. If Jonah would have just been obedient THE FIRST TIME, he would have never seen the inside of a whale's belly. But, through God's loving chastisement, Jonah was OBEDIENT when the voice of the Lord came THE **SECOND** time.

Isn't that just how we are even today? We believe that our way is the better way. We believe that what we feel in our hearts is the way we are to react. We believe that what we see right in front of us is the ultimate reality. But how many of us know and realize that life isn't based on what we believe? Life isn't based on what we feel and life surely isn't based solely on what we see right in front of us. Remember, once God has set the stage, we have no choice but to be obedient players for the Lord. Whether His plan for your life is to be the producer, the director, the choreographer or the makeup artist of that stage play – follow His plan for your life. This is crucial to your ultimate SUCCESS.

Through obedience we are sure to eat the good of the land. Through obedience, we are sure to enlarge our territories. Through obedience, we are certain to accomplish all things desired. Through obedience, we are certain to have SUCCESS in all of our endeavors. And yes, this even applies to business ownership.

Additionally, we are not in competition with one another. Believe me when I say that each piece of the pie is big enough for EVERYONE to receive a hefty slice. Other business owners with the same missions as ours are not our enemies. Other business owners in the same area by location are not our enemies. Competition doesn't mean adversary. Competition only comes to ensure that you stay on your toes. Competition only comes to ensure that your business is more unique than the next. Competition only comes to ensure that you remain ready and focused at all times. Remember, what God has for you is for YOU.

It doesn't matter what "Mary" down the street is doing, or what "Bob" around the corner is doing. Just focus on what God has placed in your spirit. You really won't have time to focus on anyone else. Remember, stay focused on what's growing in your own backyard. Your time will soon become your most valued commodity. So don't waste it on frivolous adventures which won't amount to anything substantial. Soon a fruitful business will be birthed from your spirit and you will be praising God for what He has done in and through YOU!! Again, your competitors are <u>not</u> your adversaries. We know that we have but <u>one</u> adversary, the devil.

<u>1 Peter 5:8</u>
Be sober, be vigilant; because your adversary the devil, as a roaring lion, walketh about, seeking whom he may devour:

All the devil does is roar AS a lion. He has NO bark and he certainly has NO bite. We must realize who he is and what he is....A LIAR!!! The truth isn't in him, so don't let him fool you into believing that he has power over your life. Don't let him fool you into believing that he has power over your finances. Don't let him fool you into believing that he has power over your family. And don't let him fool you into believing that he has power over your business. HE HAS **<u>NO</u>** POWER!!!

God's Word declares that the enemy is seeking whom he <u>MAY</u> devour. It never says that you <u>WILL</u> be devoured. Have you ever walked passed your neighbor's yard and your neighbor's dog is behind a locked chained fenced gate barking and barking and barking. Now, the dog knows he can't get out of the yard because the gate is locked. It doesn't stop the dog from barking anyway. All you're doing is passing your neighbor's yard. But it doesn't stop the dog from barking. Same instance occurs with the enemy. Your dreams won't stop him from trying to devour them. Your aspirations won't stop him from trying to make you believe that he has power, which he doesn't. Why do we continually give power away to the powerless? As Believers, we MUST stop giving our power away to the enemy. With God on your side, there is no way he can ever devour you and that includes your business. We must stay before the Lord so we are not ignorant to the devices of the enemy. As you are writing the vision for your business, you must remain in prayer. You will soon discover, if you haven't done so already, that prayer will definitely become your best friend, your spiritual weapon, and your fortress.

Don't be fooled by the adversary. This adversary is coming for one reason and one reason alone:

John 10:10
The thief cometh not, but for to steal, and to kill, and to destroy: I am come that they might have life, and that they might have it more abundantly
---

Don't let him steal your joy. Don't let him kill your dream. Don't let him destroy your vision. If we can only believe in God's Word, syllable by syllable, word for word, not adding anything to it and not taking anything away from it. The last portion of that verse is crucial for it states that He came so that we might have life more abundantly. Don't you want ALL that God has for you? I know I do. What He has for me is for me and no devil in hell can take it from me!! All we have to do is realize who we are in Christ!! All we have to do is realize what we mean to Christ!!! All we have to do is trust and believe that He wants us to not only grow spiritually but to also grow in land, to also grow in substance, and to also grow in perseverance.

Having our own business is such a joyous occasion in one's life. It shouldn't be trampled upon because others can't see your vision. Remember, it's not their "business" to see your vision. It's not their "business" to even understand your vision. And guess what? It isn't even their "business" to support your vision. God gave this vision to **you** for PURPOSE. God gave this vision to **you** for DESTINY. It's yours and yours alone. It is up to us to follow God's plan for our lives, in EVERY facet of our lives, which includes business ownership.

Jeremiah 29:11
For I know the thoughts that I think toward you, saith the Lord, thoughts of peace, and not of evil, to give you an expected end.

As Believers, you must know what your EXPECTED END is. As you embark upon your business venture, you never know just how many lives you can touch. You will never know just how many lives can be impacted just from a friendly smile. Your business is also your ministry. That is your EXPECTED END – to win souls to Christ and to do that which God has called you to do. That is your expected end. Just know that every facet of your life is designed to please the Father.

Hebrews 11:1
Now faith is the substance of things hoped for, the evidence of things not seen.

As Believers, it is extremely important that we exercise our faith. Faith is believing THAT you know. Faith is believing WHAT you know and Faith is standing firmly on that knowledge. Don't be waivered in your faith. It doesn't matter what it looks like naturally. Believe me when I tell you, I know!!! All hell can be breaking loose around you, but STAND FIRM in what you believe.

Our natural eyes never saw Jesus perform any of the miracles described in the Bible. We never saw Jesus cure diseases, make the lame walk, or make the blind see. We never actually saw Jesus hanging on the cross. We believe those things through our Faith. Remember what He told Thomas?

> ***John 20:29***
> *... blessed are they that have not seen, and yet have believed.*

This is the actual exercising of our faith. Believing without actually having seen PROOF!!! Thomas saw Jesus. He saw the holes in His hands. Yet, he still had to place his fingers inside the holes to make sure he actually SAW WHAT HE SAW. Thomas needed PROOF that it was Jesus, and that He was raised from the dead. But blessed are they that have NOT seen, yet still believe. That's US!!! We must have faith to believe all that God has said concerning our lives. Do you want to please God?

> ***Hebrews 11:6***
> *But without faith it is impossible to please him: ...*

Just believe. Believe that your business will come into fruition. Believe that your business will be one of a kind. Believe that your business will be successful. Believe that your business will be filled with professionalism and integrity. Believe that your business will be the legacy left for your children and their children. BELIEVE!!! Faith can move mountains just by our words alone. There is so much power in what we believe as Christians.

Matthew 9:29
... According to your faith be it unto you.

It will be done unto you according to your faith. I can believe in the success of your business all day long. I can believe that you will leave that legacy for your children. I can believe that you will finish what you've started. But if YOU don't believe it, then my believing isn't worth much. You have to believe it for yourself. This is the time to exercise YOUR faith. It doesn't take much.

Remember, the Word declares that our faith only has to be the size of a mustard seed.

Matthew 17:19
And Jesus said unto them, ... If ye have faith as a grain of mustard seed, ye shall say unto this mountain, Remove hence to yonder place; and it shall remove; and nothing shall be impossible unto you.

Have you ever seen a mustard seed? It is extremely tiny. It can actually fit on the tip of your finger. This is all you need to please God. But it must be exercised. Let's compare Faith to a muscle.

You first come to the realization that you need to exercise because clothes aren't fitting as they once did or you find yourself tiring easily. You find a gym that's either close to your house that offers a great rate, convenient hours, and offers personal assistance.

After doing all this research, you finally decide to join. Your first week, you do a simple cardio workout. The second week, you initiate a full upper body workout. You now begin to feel the effects of that workout, as muscles start aching. Doing a simple chore of brushing your teeth reminds you that those muscles have been working.

The next week, you incorporate a lower body routine. You now begin to feel the effects of that workout as well, as simple standing from a seated position becomes reminiscent of that work out. Before you know it, you will be healthier, stronger and more disciplined. All in all, this workout will make you healthier and stronger PHYSICALLY. For, along with that exercise regimen comes stricter and healthier eating regimes. So it is with our Faith.

You must also exercise your Faith, knowing that it will make you spiritually healthier and stronger. Exercise doesn't always feel good, but it's necessary in order to achieve the desired outcome. The more you exercise your faith, the stronger you become. So when our adversary, the devil, comes in with those attacks, you'll be well equipped to place him under your feet. You'll be well equipped to send him back to the pit from whence he came and where he will surely return.

James 2:17
Even so faith, if it hath not works, is dead, being alone.

James 2:20
But wilt thou know, O vain main, that faith without works is dead?

James 2:26
For as the body without the spirit is dead, so faith without works is dead also...

James speaks on this topic in three different places within the SAME chapter. Does it now get your attention? Faith is an action word. That business will NOT fall from the sky into your lap. I wish it did, but it doesn't, and it WON'T. You have to DO SOMETHING. What that something is depends solely on you. This is not a "get-rich-quick" scheme or a fancy gimmick. This is not something that you practice for a fleeting moment and then fall right back into old habits. This is a way of life. And this way of life will ensure SUCCESS for the rest of your life, inclusive of ANY business venture you desire.

One thing that I've learned through this entrepreneurial walk with God is the unfortunate fact that not everyone can handle what God has given you. You have dreams of business ownership. And you fully understand just how important this dream is to you and how important it is to your family. Others may not be able to fully comprehend just how important this is to you.

Your vision can definitely become a reality but you must first learn when to speak and when to keep quiet. It may not be time yet to speak on such things. Just write your vision. Don't speak your vision until God reveals the time to speak it.

Remember Joseph? Joseph was a dreamer and he was also able to interpret dreams. This was a gift of God given only to him. Now, why wouldn't his brothers be happy and rejoice that God gave him such an awesome gift? JEALOUSY. Jealousy creeps "her" head in just as a snake slithers across the floor.

Jealousy of others is a core reason why most business owners won't go forward with what God has planted on the insides of them. You tell your dreams to people because you're so excited. You tell your dreams to people because you want them to be just as excited for you. After all, these are some of the same people claiming to be your lifelong supporters. These are some of the same people claiming to love you unconditionally. Keep your mouth shut!!! Ask God to reveal to you those persons who are truly and sincerely happy for you. Ask God to reveal to you those persons who will be truly praying for your success. Otherwise, KEEP YOUR TRAP SHUT. Always be quick to hear and slow to speak.

Additionally, don't be overly concerned by what's going on around you. So what if it looks like businesses are failing around you. So what if businesses have GRAND OPENINGS today and GRAND CLOSINGS next month. We are not to live our lives by what we see anyway. Are you not exercising your faith?

Are you lined up with God's will for your life? As Believers, we walk by our faith and not with what our natural eyes behold. Always hold on to what God's Word declares for your life, and watch how it shall manifest itself in your life.

So, just know that during this entrepreneurial walk, doors will close in your face. Some doors will even SLAM shut in your face. But never lose heart and don't become discouraged. Even King David stated that there have been times that he had to encourage himself. Learn to speak those things over your life aimed at ultimate SUCCESS!!!

When those doors slam shut in your face, maybe, just maybe, it's a door that you are persistently trying to walk through, while God, Himself, purposely closed that door for your good. Don't try to go through a door that God has closed. You are sure to shipwreck yourself and your business before it ever gets started.

2

MINDSET CHANGE

We clearly have to change the way we think about EVERYTHING to be entrepreneurs. This is so important for ultimate SUCCESS. Remember, we're moving from an Employee mentality to an Employer mentality and it takes a lot sometimes to transfer from one to the other. We have to always see the glass as half full instead of viewing it as half empty. And we have to take adversity as a clear challenge that better is on the horizon. If we don't change the way we think, then business ownership will remain a dream and will never see the light of day. If we don't change the way we think, then wealth will only be a "what if I had" instead of a "thank God I have."

We have to know that we know what we know. It's just that simple. Know who you are. Know whose you are. Do you know for a certainty that God loves you? Do you know without a shadow of a doubt that Christ died for YOU? You must continually say what God says. You must continually say what God says concerning your life.

God thinks good thoughts of us continually. Now, if He can think good of us, why then can't we think good of ourselves? We must change the way we think about ourselves. Have we been perfect? No. Have we done it ALL right? No. Ask for God's forgiveness and then forgive yourself. He has so much in store for you and for your business. Take Him at His Word!!!

With God by your side, there's nothing you can't do. As a matter of fact, the word "CAN'T" should not exist within your vocabulary. God has equipped us to SUCCEED. Failure is NEVER an option. Any task set before us is an already conquered task. The only way this will become a manifested part of your life is that you MUST believe it to be so. Change your mindset and you can change your situation. Change your mindset and you can change your circumstance. Change the way you think about things and you can change your life.

Philippians 2:5
Let this mind be in you, which was also in Christ Jesus:

There are so many passages of scripture which teaches us to change our mindset. We transform ourselves through the renewing of our mind.

Romans 12:2
And be not conformed to this world: but be ye transformed by the renewing of your mind, that ye may prove what is good, and acceptable, and perfect, will of God.

What does it mean to transform? To transform means to make a DRAMATIC and thorough CHANGE. If something is THOROUGH it means that it is complete in EVERY detail. It means that no stone was left unturned.

What does it mean to renew? To renew means to make like new, to restore, to make fresh. If something has to be restored, then it means that that something had a flaw in it in some way. In order for something to be restored, it must have been tainted or destroyed in some way. To restore means to bring it back to its original condition or state.

> ***1 Corinthians 15:57***
> *But thank be to God, which giveth us the victory through our Lord Jesus Christ.*

God's Word declares that we are victorious over everything. Did you know that everything incorporates and includes your business? If you want God's Word to work in your life, then you have to be obedient to His Word. You cannot expect His Word to have its full effect in your life if you are not willing to allow it to become the true building blocks or the foundation for your life.

He gives us the power to get wealth. He's the one who gives us the witty ideas to create businesses. Only through Him will these ideas become a reality in our lives. See yourself as God sees you. You are VICTORIOUS in your business. Your business will SUCCEED. I will have the necessary FAITH as that of a mustard seed to move that mountain completely out of my way.

Believe what He says about your life concerning your business. He will never leave you, nor forsake you. Keep Him first, as the center of ALL things, and watch Him do it on your behalf. That's the kind of God we serve.

He even declares to us that we are not going to be the ones borrowing but, in fact, we will be lending to those needing assistance.

Deuteronomy 28:12-13
The Lord shall open unto thee his good treasure, . . . and thou shalt lend unto many nations, and thou shalt not borrow.

And the Lord shall make thee the head, and not the tail; and thou shalt be above only, and thou shalt not be beneath; ...

He shall make us the head and not the tail. See, this is what I was alluding to earlier. We have to see ourselves as God sees us. We have to speak those things over our lives that are in accordance with God's Word.

It is extremely important to be very careful of what you speak. What you speak concerning your life, the lives of others and even concerning your business can have lasting effects, whether positive or negative.

Proverbs 18:21
Death and life are in the power of the tongue . . .

If you want that business to SUCCEED, then speak SUCCESS over that business. If you constantly tell yourself, "I don't have the money to get the business started", then, guess what? The business won't get started. If you constantly tell yourself, "I don't know the first thing about starting a business", then, guess what? You will never gain the knowledge you need to start a business. Stop talking yourself out of business ownership. The world understands this principal. Why are the Believers still speaking damnation into their lives? We have the power on the inside of us to literally change our situation. Utilize what God has placed on the inside of you. It's there for a reason.

You want that business to succeed? Start saying this, "In the name of Jesus, my business will succeed. In the name of Jesus, I will obtain the knowledge that I need to SUCCESSfully open and maintain my business. In the name of Jesus, God will prepare me for the things which are to come." Watch God do it!

You must put this member (the tongue) under subjection to what God's plan is for your life. You may not currently have a business, but SPEAK as business owners speak. You may not have your first million yet, but SPEAK as millionaires speak. Surround yourself with people speaking the same language you speak. Get rid of the dead weight!!! I use this analogy all the time:

The SUCCESS TRAIN 2015 started out of the gate on January 1, 2015. I decided to get on that train. Now, unfortunately, others also got on that train. These "others" were trying to slow the train down because it was moving entirely too fast for them. These "others" began getting motion sickness because they couldn't handle the speed of the train. It is not your job to comfort them during this time. It is not your job to have the conductor slow the train down. It is ONLY your job to continue on the path God has set your feet upon. If the train is going too fast, then maybe these "others" weren't ready to jump on board.

They must recognize that the train is going too fast. Once this realization hits, they should just JUMP OFF. Don't slow the train down because it's too fast for you. You will hinder others who are ready for the speed the train is taking.

So, in other words, don't let anyone hinder your forward progress. You may stop to help them and never get back on track. Pray for them and keep it moving.

Remember, we discussed how to change your thought pattern? Always remember that the devil can put all sorts of thoughts into your head. "Business ownership isn't for me." "It's too hard to start a business." "I don't have enough money to start a business." "I'm not smart enough to start a business." Remember, you have to change your thinking. You must put on the mind of Christ. If God is giving you the vision, then I promise you He will also give the PROVISIONS for the vision.

If your circle includes people who are satisfied with just EXISTING rather than LIVING, then those are the people you need to cut off completely. These people are also a part of the "others" that were on your train. You must keep your circle FREE OF DEBRIS. Okay, I will repeat that. You MUST keep your circle FREE OF DEBRIS. Debris can come in any form, any shape and in any situation. Question is: Do you have the ability to recognize debris? Or, are you trying to filter the debris to make it more palatable in your life?

It is now your time to start living and not merely existing. It is now your time to grab hold of all God has in store for you. You've allowed the devil to take, rob, kill and destroy your dreams for far too long. Are you willing to take that first step into financial freedom? Are you willing to take that first step into enlarging your territory? Are you willing to take that first step into empowered entrepreneurship? Are you willing to take that first step into wealth building and knowledge? Are you willing to take that first step into the rest of your life?

3

IS IT RIGHT FOR YOU??

So often, people ask this very question: "Is business ownership right for them?" This is a great question for introspection. Ask yourself this question over and over again.

Unfortunately, business ownership isn't for everyone. You have to be passionate about your business. The passion regarding your business is what's going to sustain that business during tough times. Your passion regarding a business is the very thing that will keep you motivated to endure the rough trials that are sure to come. Business ownership isn't easy. It takes a special person to become, not only an entrepreneur, but a self-sustaining entrepreneur. If starting a business is not a passion for you, then, no, business ownership is not right for you.

The first five years of business ownership are difficult years. You may see a profit, or you may not. Those first few years will be your phase of "trial and error." Making mistakes is all a part of business ownership. But it's the only way you will truly learn your art!! Yes, business ownership is a form of art. And only those who truly want to perfect their craft will SUCCEED.

However, if during those first few years, you actually see a profit, it may not be much of one. If this business is truly not a passion of yours, then you will quit before you even get your foot out of the starting gate. Quit is NOT in the vocabulary of an entrepreneur. Quit is NOT an option for the business owner. You must endure this thing. You have to in order to have the best possible outcome.

Don't ever start a business solely based upon the belief that it will make money. Remember, I just said that most businesses will not show a profit during the first five years. During this time, you will probably just be breaking even, at best. Obviously, making money is a reason to start a business but it shouldn't be the ONLY reason. If you are starting a business ONLY to make money, then your business won't SUCCEED.

If you are passionate about something, then you will stay focused and stay true to the course. Nothing will derail you from seeing it through. Nothing will ever make you suspect that you've made a wrong move in starting this business. Your passion for this business is what's going to ensure SUCCESS.

Your passion is what truly births a business. You can become passionate about a hobby and BOOM, it becomes a business. You can become passionate about a negative encounter you just had in a retail store and BOOM, it becomes a business. That negative encounter creates a business that now solves a problem. You can become passionate about researching information, any kind of information, and BOOM, it becomes a business. Passion will birth a business. Passion will sustain a business. Passion will nurture a business. Passion will breathe life into a business.

Business ownership is very serious. Here are a few helpful hints to ponder when asking oneself if business ownership is right for you. Here are just a few helpful insights into business ownership.

> **IF YOU ARE NOT WILLING TO PUT IN THE TIME AND THE WORK, THEN BUSINESS OWNERSHIP IS <u>NOT</u> FOR YOU.**

Business ownership is a very demanding profession. It's extremely easy to get up, go to work, get off at 5:00 p.m. and go home. You don't take work home and you don't think about the office until the next day. Not quite so with business ownership. You will eat, sleep, drink and literally bathe in your business. Ideas will become a constant train of moving thoughts, which will ultimately begin to take the forms of business manuals - best practices and procedures, etc. Initially, you will be the "go-to" person for EVERYTHING. It takes a lot of time, energy, blood, sweat, and tears to become SUCCESSFUL at owning a business. As stated earlier, this is not a "get-rich-quick" scheme or a gimmick. SUCCESS won't happen overnight.

Birthing a business literally means days, weeks, months and sometimes years of painstakingly writing the vision and making it plain. You will have sleepless nights. It's part of the process. You will have long days where you feel there isn't enough time in the day to complete everything. It's part of the process. You will certainly have to become the manager, the janitor, the secretary, the receptionist, the file clerk, the payroll clerk, and even the tax professional. Again, it's part of the process. TRUST THE PROCESS!! BELIEVE IN THE PROCESS!!

Just know that your labor pains, that labor of love will become quite evident as you start seeing the fruits of that labor become ready for the harvest.

> **IF YOU ARE NOT WILLING TO MAKE THE NECESSARY SACRIFICES AND TO PRACTICE DISCIPLINE OVER YOUR FINANCES, THEN BUSINESS OWNERSHIP IS NOT FOR YOU.**

While I hate to be the bearer of bad news, I wouldn't be a person of integrity if I didn't provide ALL the facts as it relates to business ownership.

Did you know that for the first five years of opening your business, you may NOT be able to take a vacation? You can't because for those first few years, your business is YOU!! If you leave, you won't make any money. If you don't answer the phones, then you miss out on that potential customer or client. If you leave, your business will shortly come to a screeching halt.

Did you know that you probably won't be able to go shopping as often as you once did? Shopping will be a thing of the past, unless you are purchasing supplies and equipment for your business. It may not feel like it at the time, but shopping is a small sacrifice to make. Thank God for what you have and concentrate your financial efforts and discipline on building your business. It's not a hard thing to do. You have to just MAKE yourself do it and stick to it. Basically, create a budget and stick to it.

Did you know that you may have to eat peanut butter and jelly sandwiches for lunch? A PBJ sandwich with a cold glass of milk certainly will do a body good. TRUST THE PROCESS. Don't waste money on eating out when you can cook dinner and then have that dinner for lunch the next day. It's called a sacrifice. Please discipline yourselves with your finances. If you start this practice early on, then it won't feel like a burden you've placed on yourself.

These sacrifices are quite necessary (as well as many others) if you want to achieve SUCCESS in your business. These sacrifices will ultimately become a part of your daily routine. Remember, your passion has birthed a business. As parents, don't we make the necessary sacrifices for our children? Will you purchase a new pair of shoes for yourself while your child has holes in the soles of his shoes? No!! That would make you a bad and horrible parent. So it is just the same with your business. Treat your business as lovingly as you would that child. If you raise your child with morals and values, that child will grow to make you extremely proud. Again, so it is with your business. Treat your business in the same manner and when it's matured, it will make you extremely proud.

Now, this is the part that I will lose most of you. You have to be DISCIPLINED in order to be a business owner. You have to know that **AFTER** PAYING TITHES, a lot of the monies will have to go back into your business. You may NOT be able to get your nails done as often. You may NOT be able to purchase the most expensive computer. You may NOT be able to do traditional marketing and advertising. One thing I have learned is that although you have caviar taste (and it's okay to want the finer things in life) - you cannot enjoy the taste of CAVIAR on a BOLOGNA SANDWICH budget. It just doesn't work that way.

You have to become wise with your spending when starting a business.

It is also extremely important to reduce your overhead as much as possible when first starting out. It may be feasible to keep your home office initially, versus finding office space, paying rent, utilities, and other expenses when your company's model hasn't proven viable at the moment. Remember, preparing a business plan will assist in the overall planning and structure of your business. We'll discuss this at some length later on.

> **IF YOU ARE NOT WILLING TO LOSE SOME SLEEP DURING THE PROCESS, THEN BUSINESS OWNERSHIP IS <u>NOT</u> FOR YOU.**

Did you know that you may lose countless hours of sleep during this process? There have been times when God has literally awakened me in the middle of the night with fresh new ideas. Once those ideas were placed into my spirit, it was virtually impossible to return to the comfort of my bed, for I was literally on fire, so excited for what God had just planted within me. Be prepared for those kinds of nights.

Also, prepare yourself to lose sleep because of running your own business. If you are used to having a 9 to 5 job, leaving at 5, then you will be in for a rude awakening. This is YOUR business. You must treat it as a tender baby. In the beginning, that is EXACTLY what it will be to you, a baby. You will have to feed it, bathe it, clothe it, but most importantly, you will have to nurture it. No longer will you have days ending at 5 p.m. You will have days ending at midnight and sometimes into the wee hours of the morning; only to get up the next day and start the trend all over again. It is a sacrifice but it's a sacrifice worth making. There's nothing like being your own boss. But please remember that being your own boss comes with a lot of requirements. This is something that has been placed into your hands. Much is being given to you; therefore, much will be required of you. There is a cost to be the boss.

Just as a baby wakes up in the middle of the night, same will be for your business. Just as a baby needs love and affection, same will be for your business. Just as a baby needs nutrition, shelter and love, the same will be for your business.

GET READY!!! GET READY!!! GET READY!!!

When you see your baby reach adulthood, degree in hand, then you know it was well worth those sleepless nights. This is also true for your business. When you start seeing those incredible profits coming through the door exemplified by thousands of satisfied customers, and vacationing to exotic destinations, you will be able to say that those sleepless nights were well worth the sacrifice.

> **IF YOU ARE NOT WILLING TO HELP OTHERS ALONG THE WAY, ALLOWING YOUR ROAD TO <u>SUCCESS</u> TO BECOME THE STEPPING STONE FOR SOMEONE ELSE, THEN BUSINESS OWNERSHIP IS <u>NOT</u> FOR YOU.**

Selfishness is a sure sign that your business will not SUCCEED. Always saying "I" versus "We" and "Us" is a sure fire way of ensuring the destruction of your business. Remember, the title of this book is "It's God's Business: Your Road to Success." If God is giving you all the tools needed for SUCCESS, then please know that selfishness is not part of His equation.

You must be able to help someone else. Let them know of the pitfalls you were subject to overcome. It may help them not to succumb to those same pits. Your help may just be the catalyst they need for motivation and encouragement. As stated earlier, remember, we are not in competition with one another. The slices of the pie are big enough for everyone.

We have to be in a position to help someone else. God's principles will not allow you to have the mentality of "I got mine, now get yours." God will allow you to "get yours" only in furthering His agenda, His kingdom. Business ownership is a wonderful tool to master. Business ownership is a vehicle whereby God's glory can truly be seen. Why would you NOT help someone else's dream become reality? Just try it and see how marvelously He blesses you and crowns all your efforts with SUCCESS!!!!

4

PROSPERITY PLAN

Of course God wants you to prosper. Remember, He thinks of good things when He thinks of us. Why wouldn't He want you to prosper right here on earth? He has stored up treasures for us in heaven, and I thank God for those treasures. Those heavenly treasures are our ultimate possessions. Those heavenly treasures will certainly be a sight to behold. But we also have earthen treasures that we can enjoy NOW.

> **_III John 1:2_**
> *Beloved, I wish above all things that thou mayest prosper and be in health, even as thy soul prospers.*

God wants His people to be prosperous AS the soul prospers. This shows us that God is concerned about the TOTAL man, not just one aspect of his being. It is extremely important to have the things you need and it's a wonderful thing to be able to enjoy some luxuries, but isn't it more important to ensure the prosperity of your soul?

> **_Mark 8:36_**
> *For what shall it profit a man, if he shall gain the whole world, and lose his own soul?*

It is a fact that we were born with nothing. It is even more of a fact that when we die, we will die also with nothing. When you die and are buried, your diamond ring, your Rolex, and your Maserati will not be standing before the Lord in judgment. You and you alone will stand before Him.

God is still in the blessing business. He has NEVER fallen short of what He wants to do for His people. We are the ones who fall short in obtaining His many blessings. Now, if you follow God's principles for your life and for your business, you will surely prosper. It's in His Word and God's Word can't lie. Now, please be sure to not forget where those blessings came from. Just because you have been blessed MORE THAN MEASURE doesn't mean you stop going to church, or stop praying, or stop fasting, or stop giving God true reverence. Remember this as well:

Job 1:21
. . . the Lord giveth, and the Lord hath taken away...

Never allow the blessings to make you forget the BLESSER. Never allow the blessings to make you lose sight of the real reason for the blessing: TO BE A BLESSING TO SOMEONE ELSE!! And to further God's Kingdom!! Yes, you are to build wealth, but ensure that the wealth doesn't build you into something that God doesn't recognize.

Proverbs 13:22
A good man leaveth an inheritance to his children's children: and the wealth of the sinner is laid up for the just.

If God's plan for your business wasn't to build wealth, then why would He tell us that the wealth of this world is laid up for us? What that means is that you can have your slice of the pie. That slice can be large enough to encompass your dreams and the dreams of your children and the dreams of your grandchildren. Just because you come from an impoverished family doesn't mean that you can't be the one to break this vicious cycle. It can all start with YOU!!!

Okay, now, let's get this right. Do you need money to effectively run a business? Yes. Do you need money to live? Yes. Do you just need money? Yes. We need money to live. We need money to survive? Right? It's not the money that's the problem. It's the **LOVE** of the money that creates the problem.

<u>I Timothy 6:10</u>
For the love of money is the root of all evil . . .

When you would do anything, hurt anyone, lie, cheat, steal or kill just to get money, then, yes, you have a problem. Money has now become your god.

God's people were MEANT to be wealthy. Job was wealthy. Abraham was wealthy. Lot was wealthy. Daniel was wealthy. David (oops, King David) was wealthy. These people had powerful positions. Let me rephrase that – these people were BLESSED with powerful positions. So, wealth is meant for us. Just make sure that you don't love and desire the wealth more than you love and desire God!!!!

Who wouldn't want to have an abundant life? Most of us are not living abundantly because we have totally taken God out of the equation. God is the "equal sign" for all things.

Prayer + Fasting = Breakthrough

Through prayer and fasting you will reach the breakthrough that only God can give.

You must seek God while He can yet be found. Take time to spend with God. Get a relationship with Him. I used to hear the elder generation say that it's sweeter than the honey in a honeycomb. Now that I know Him for myself, I concur. Loving God has been my greatest accomplishment. It is so sweet to be in commune with Him.

Matthew 6:33
But seek he first the kingdom of God, and his righteousness; and all these things shall be added unto you.

Don't seek Him for what He can do for you. Seek Him because it's the only thing that you CAN do. Seek Him with your whole heart and watch those businesses grow. Seek Him in every aspect of that business from the business name to the business location, and watch that business grow. Keep Him as the center of all things and watch prosperity come knocking at your door.

Proverbs 3:6
In all thy ways acknowledge him, and he shall direct thy paths.

What better direction to get than direction from the Almighty? You don't know what to do, or which way to go? Just acknowledge that He is God. Besides God, there is none other. He is the only true and living God. We can do nothing without Him. Just tell Him how wonderful He is. Tell Him how much you love and adore Him. After all, He is WORTHY of all the glory, of all the honor, and of all the praise. Even if you had 10,000 tongues, it still wouldn't be enough to exalt Him just for being God.

Malachi 3:8-10
Will a man rob God? Yet ye have robbed me. But ye say, Wherein have we robbed thee? In tithes and offerings.

Ye are cursed with a curse: for ye have robbed me, even this whole nation.

Bring ye all the tithes into the storehouse, that there may be meat in mine house, and prove me now herewith, saith the Lord of hosts, if I will not open you the windows of heaven, and pour you out a blessing, that there shall not be room enough to receive it.

Pay your tithes. Please do not forget to pay your tithes. Did I mention that it was extremely important to pay your tithes? I can't stress this enough. Please pay your tithes and watch God bless you. I'm a living witness that this holy obligation works. If I only made one dollar, I made sure God received His ten cents. You are only giving back to God what is His anyway. Please don't rob God of what is rightfully His. As your business makes money, please make sure that He receives a tenth from that income off the top.

I've heard so many people use these excuses for not paying tithes: "The Preacher is rich enough." "He's only going to use the money to buy another car." "He can't tell me how much to give." "He will only use the money for his personal gain, not for the church."

Well, let me immediately dispel some of these crazy notions and ideologies that so many of us have either heard or maybe even believe.

Proverbs 3:9-10
Honour the Lord with thy substance, and with the firstfruits of all thine increase: So shall thy barns be filled with plenty, and thy presses shall burst out with new wine.

First of all, no man can give you a mandate to do anything in God's house. This mandate to honor God with your substance and first fruits, to pay tithes, and specifically, to pay a tenth of your earnings, comes from God Himself. No preacher is mandating anything. This is a sacred command coming from God.

Next, our only position should be to obey God. Now, if the preacher is squandering all the money, then God will deal justly with that preacher. It isn't in our power to determine what is or what is not happening with the tithes you have paid to God's kingdom <u>out of obedience</u>. Now, if you are having your doubts as to whether or not the preacher is mishandling church money then pray and talk to God about it. Seek His face as to whether or not you should still belong to that particular church. Maybe it is time to find another church home, or maybe the preacher is actually handling God's money honestly. Sometimes God will give a mandate to the preacher that maybe the flock can't understand. Remember, everything that is done in the dark will come to the light. Just stand still, continue YOUR obedience to God and allow God to deal justly with that preacher.

Let's just say that the preacher is squandering the money!! If you are faithfully paying your tithes as God has commanded, you will still reap the benefits of having done so; regardless of how the "preacher" appropriates those funds. We pay tithes because of God's commandment, not because of the preacher.

If we just follow God's Prosperity Plan, we will certainly experience monetary success, physical health and spiritual growth. I certainly believe that with all three of these things, SUCCESS is an ultimate outcome. This is the PERFECT and ONLY prosperity plan!!! And don't let anyone dictate otherwise.

Remember, all you have to do is plant the seed. God's Word tells us that we are like a tree, planted by the rivers of water. That seed that you've planted will take root. And because of the fact that this seed has an endless stream of water to nourish it, an endless stream of water to cultivate it, and an endless stream of water to secure it in its proper place – watch that seed take root and grow to its utmost potential. Just plant the seed and watch God give the increase.

5

FEAR FACTOR

It is true and most certainly accurate that most businesses are not created due to FEAR. If fear is the precursor to your business, then fear will embed the creative process. Fear will embed the developmental phase. Fear will cripple any start-up efforts. And fear will leave its marked stamp of approval that your business is doomed to fail. You must rid yourself of the fear factor. What are you afraid of? No, really?? What are you afraid of? Are you afraid that your business just might produce millions in revenue? Are you afraid of actual SUCCESS?

Fear will cause us to miss out on that abundant life that God has waiting for us. Fear will cause us to become hesitant to move. Fear will cause us to procrastinate when we know beyond a shadow of a doubt that God's voice proclaimed, **"Go!!"** Fear can become a fathom power, if we let it. Did you catch that? Fear can become a _**fathom**_ power, if you let it.

Just what is a "fathom" power? To fathom something means that you have an understanding of it or you have an explanation for it. This "understanding" and "explanation", then, allows this "it" to become clear and concise. Fear is something that should be totally unexplainable because it's something that God didn't give us. Fear is something that shouldn't be understood, for it is that which we shouldn't want. Fear is something that is totally unclear because it shouldn't be a part of our framework. Fear should be so far removed from us because of our constant walking in the light of God's love and in the hopes of all His promises. We cannot allow fear to become a part of our makeup. We cannot allow fear to become a soothing cop-out. We cannot allow fear to juxtapose our positioning within the Kingdom.

Fear can quickly become so inert within us that it begins to take on our very fabric. It begins to look like us. We become so comfortable and complacent with fear riding our shoulders that without it, we can't even recognize our own reflection in the mirror. Our reflection takes on this hideous caricature instead of that reflection emulating our Creator, God the Father. When we look in the mirror, is it fear we see, or is it God's plan that we are envisioning?

We have already established that God is constantly with us. We have already established that God will never leave nor will He ever forsake us. We have already established that what God has for us, it is for us and no one can ever take it away. We have already established that God's thoughts towards us are of good and not of evil. We have already established that God not only wants us to prosper, but He EXPECTS that we do so.

We discussed earlier how to exercise our faith. Faith and fear cannot co-exist. It's like oil and water. Oil and water will never intertwine to become one entity. It just won't happen. You can try your best to introduce oil to water. You can try your best to introduce water to oil. Shake it as abruptly and as vigorously as humanly possible. As soon as the container is left to rest, you will IMMEDIATELY see the oil separate itself from the water. The two cannot exist as one unified solution. It will NEVER happen. So it is with your faith. Fear will NEVER unify itself with your faith. And Faith will NEVER unify with fear.

God will always be with us, no matter where we go, and no matter what we do. So, why do we allow fear to slither in like a snake hunting its prey? It is DEFINITELY something that WE allow in our lives. Fear is not what God had in mind for us and it certainly isn't anything that He, himself, gives to us.

II Timothy 1:7
For God hath not given us the spirit of fear; but of power, and of love, and of a sound mind.

God has bestowed upon us Power, Love and a Sound Mind. This Power enables us to believe in His truths. This Power allows us to forgive what we once believed to be unforgiveable. This Power allows us to Love unconditionally in and out of season. This Power allows us to love even when agape love is unfashionable. This Power restores our thoughts, restores our ability to know and to believe that with God all things are possible. Once fear grips you, its hold can become relentless. Its hold is one that can bound you so tightly that you begin to believe it to be the norm, the way it should be, the very foundation of everything you hold dear and near to your heart.

Remember, if you fear everything and if you will allow fear to totally dictate your every move (or lack thereof), then how is your faith fully operational? It's the same premise as worry and prayer. If you are going to worry about everything, then there's no need to pray. And if you are earnestly praying about everything, then why are you worrying? Is God not such that He answers prayer? Is God not such that He gives us everything we need in this life to prosper, to be in good health and even to tame the devil?

Matthew 9:29
"... According to your faith, be it unto you."

Everything will be unto you as your faith allows. If you have not exercised your faith, then you are no better than a 90-pound weakling, trying to fight the giants, but not having enough strength to pull it off. Please do not allow fear to grip you and smother your voice. Do not allow fear to suddenly attack your mind that you refuse to move forward. Seasons change and so must we. But if fear has a lock on your transition then you will remain stagnant in whatever season you're currently exposed to without any sight of a pleasant oasis.

6

MAKE IT LEGAL

It is imperative that businesses are formed LEGALLY. The days of "pay me under the table" are long gone, or those days SHOULD be long gone. We talk about the blessings of God, how we want those blessings to overtake us, to overshadow us. However, legally forming a business is the last thing on anyone's agenda. We have all heard the phrase, "God won't bless your mess." This saying is so very true. If you are not handling your business appropriately and honestly WITH YOURSELF, then how can you expect to handle it appropriately and honestly with any prospective clients?

If you have not taken the time to form legal credentials: a Sole Proprietorship, a Corporation, a Limited Liability Company, or some sort of Partnership, then guess what? You are not being honest with yourself. If you are selling CD's out of your trunk and you are lacking any one of these credentials, then you are NOT a business. You are a hustler in businessman's clothing and it will eventually come to light. In order for any of these Godly principles to take root in your life then you must do EVERYTHING God's way.

__Mark 12:17__
And Jesus answering said unto them, Render to Caesar the things that are Caesar's, and to God, the things that are God's.

Everyone, for some reason, is afraid of paying taxes. You want your slice of the pie (and a big slice, I might add). You want the American Dream. Well, part of that American Dream is to pay your portion of American Taxes. If God is blessing your business to the degree of your having to pay Uncle Sam his portion, then isn't it likely to assume that you will be making enough money to actually PAY those taxes? My God, if you owe Uncle Sam $10,000 in taxes, can you imagine how much revenue your business made over the course of that year? (Just a little food for thought.)

All states have certain statutes and regulations in order to obtain a license and/or permit to engage in certain businesses. It is your responsibility to familiarize yourself with these statutes and regulations BEFORE opening a business. For example, you will need a license, certifications, and will also have to follow certain rules and regulations in order to operate a daycare facility. In some states, even barbers, hair stylists, funeral directors and a host of other businesses will have to be licensed and certified before being able to operate their respective businesses. The type of businesses subject to these licensing requirements varies from state to state and it is totally **your** responsibility to ensure that your business falls or doesn't fall in this category. Check with your state's Secretary of State for further information.

Have you considered starting a business right from your home? Obviously, starting a business at home comes with lots of pluses and perks. You are probably comfortable there, the price is affordable, and you can dress as casually as you'd like. But just because it's your PC in your den doesn't necessarily mean you have the right to do whatever you want. There are a few legal hurdles to clear if you're starting a home-based business, as well as tax deductions, licenses and certifications you must still consider. We are not purporting to be tax professionals but we will recommend that you seek the consultation of one as soon as possible. As usual, it's better to deal with these issues now rather than later. Shuffling them off to the back of your mind or the bottom of the "to-do" pile might lead to trouble and hassles later on.

Do you know the differences between the various business entities? Below is just a brief overview of the different types of business entities. You can use this as quick peek into what could be yours.

These are just basic definitions of the various types of business entities, or "credentials" as they were previously referred to. Again, please note that we are not tax professionals. We are simply providing information. We recommend contacting your local CPA or tax professional for the tax ramifications associated with each type of business entity.

Sole Proprietorship: A proprietorship is formed when an individual (or proprietor) forms a business without the protection afforded to corporations and/or limited liability companies. Normally, when a business is formed, it becomes a separate entity from the owner. Not so with a sole proprietorship. This form of business has no separate identity (or legal existence) apart from the proprietor. An example of this would be John Doe d/b/a Freedom Services. If Freedom Services is sued for any reason, John Doe will be the person sued. John Doe then runs the risk of losing all personal assets. The advantages to a sole proprietorship is that its more cost effective and there are no formalities involved. However, it doesn't afford the owner any protection.

Corporation: A corporation is a company distinct from its individual owner(s) and provides legal and liability protections.

Limited Liability Company: A limited liability company, like a corporation, is completely distinct from its individual owner(s) and provides legal and liability protections.

Partnership: A partnership is a contract by which a company is formed whereby person(s) delineate the percentage of ownership had by each and also delineates the duties and responsibilities of each partner.

Non-profit Corporation: A non-profit corporation is an entity separate from its individual owner, created for the sole purpose of assisting a community, without the goal of personal financial gain.

Each structure of business comes with its own set of legal ramifications as well as tax issues. Once again, it is our recommendation that you consult a tax professional to choose which entity is right for you.

Once you have legally formed your business, you will need to obtain a tax I.D. number or EIN. This can be done relatively simply just by going to the IRS website and requesting to obtain your tax I.D. number online (www.irs.gov). It takes a minimum of five minutes to complete the online application. Once done, you will receive your tax I.D. letter online, which can then be saved to your computer and printed out.

Once you have determined the structure of your business and obtained the tax I.D. number from the IRS, the next important step is to make sure that what your business is offering is exactly what the community needs. Is it your goal to start a retail company selling the same shoes as the retail shoe company just one block away? Or, will you start a retail company selling the same shoes BUT with a unique twist. Always make sure that your offering is uniquely different than the next company's offering. It is important that your company has a unique edge all of its own. All this means is that your business is uniquely furnishing a customer's need. All this means is that your business is employing its passion for the unique needs of its customer base.

Although profit margins are extremely important, it isn't as important as ensuring fair pricing. You will be sure to gain repeat customers and referrals by always pricing your goods and services FAIRLY. Integrity in business is a MUST. Be fair, not greedy. Being fair will ensure wealth. Greed creates a fleeting, momentary financial gain that will soon weather the test of time. If you are not fair then you will not create a wealth of repeat customers, which is VITAL. Not only will those repeat customers continually give business, but those same repeat customers will tell everyone they know about how fair you were with them. Word of mouth is the best and the CHEAPEST form of advertising.

The next important thing is to diversify your business portfolio. What exactly does this mean? Well, let's use my company, Granting Favor Consultants, as the guinea pig.

When I started my company, Granting Favor Consultants, back in 2008, it started merely with grant writing services. I had experience writing grants prior to the start of my company and I wanted to start getting paid for my area of expertise.

In the course of obtaining customers needing grants, it came to my attention that these companies also needed to obtain 501(c)(3) tax exemption. Well, I needed to diversify my portfolio in order to attract those potential customers needing this exemption in order to be eligible to apply for grant funding.

Well, again, in the midst of assisting these companies, it was brought to my attention that for-profit businesses needed assistance just as much or maybe more than non-profit organizations. The main way to receive much needed funding for a for-profit business is through loans. How do we apply for such loans? Well, a business plan is a sure fire way of having the necessary documentation to apply for loans. Well, I have once again diversified my portfolio to include preparing professional business plans.

So, as you can see, I was open to changing my business model. By doing so, I now have created different streams of potential income within the framework of ONE business enterprise: grant writing; 501(c)(3) assistance; and business plan preparation.

Over the years, this range of diversification has grown even larger and encompasses varying aspects of recommended business practices, all of which are designed to assist ANY business in growing and prospering.

7

BRANDING

Always make sure that your business is a direct reflection of you. Everything about your business should be done decently and in order. You and your business are now considered a BRAND. Once that business is started on paper, you should be in the process of perfecting and maturing that brand. This is accomplished through business cards, letterhead, logos, websites, blogs, and, of course, social media.

Your company's brand gets noticed before you do. Your company's brand is your first line of defense. Your company's brand is the one thing that will ensure that your company is recognized before the public even knows YOUR name. You want them to know the NAME OF THE COMPANY before they realize who actually owns the company. It is just that important to start your brand and follow it through.

You can create pages for your business through Facebook, LinkedIn, Twitter, and through blogs. With modern technology ever evolving, it is essential to have an online presence. You really have NO choice. When networking with other like-minded entrepreneurs, I promise one of the top five questions you will be asked is: "Do you have a website?"

In the beginning, finances may not allow you to do extensive marketing. But you can employ what I like to call "the poor man's marketing strategies." As mentioned above, you can start your online presence through social media: Facebook, LinkedIn, and Twitter. These sites are FREE. It costs NOTHING to start a business page.

Also, you can create a logo for FREE. Some services I've found include www.freelogoservices.com; www.logogarden.com; www.logoyes.com. Now, depending on how customized you would like these logos to be will ultimately depend upon the charge. But initially, these sites are free. Just take a moment to review all these sites have to offer. Remember, BRANDING is everything.

You will also need business cards. Vista Print offers a variety of business cards for every industry out there. A large percentage of these cards are FREE. All you pay are nominal shipping charges. Again, depending on the complexity of how you want these cards to look, and if you would like to have writing on the backs of these cards will ultimately determine pricing.

Never be caught without your business cards. One thing I hate is for a business owner to promote their business and when asked for a card, the reply is, "Oh, I don't have any on me." Marketing for business owners is a 24/7 process. You will always have opportunities for customer relationships – grocery shopping, shoe shopping, manicures, pedicures, hardware stores, etc. If you hand out just one card a day, that is a potential for 365 new customers.

Also, you will want to send out email to current and potential clients. Mail Chimp is a wonderful avenue to use for free. It just takes a little time to get everything set up, but ultimately, FREE is always a great price.

8

ENDURANCE

I've stated it before and I believe this is a great time to reiterate the fact that this is NOT A GET-RICH QUICK SCHEME or a GIMMICK TO GET RICH. SUCCESS is evident but it won't happen overnight. It will happen, though, through hard work, non-compromising attitudes, perseverance, and endurance.

Ecclesiastes 9:11
I returned, and saw under the sun, that the race is not to the swift, nor the battle to the strong, . . .
Matthew 24: 13
But he that shall endure unto the end, . . .

It's perfectly okay to start out small. It doesn't matter how long it takes to get that business started. The main issue is to actually START. It's better to start slowly than to come out of the gate at full gallop only to stumble and never reach the finish line. Never underestimate the value of starting small, especially if your resources dictate such. Here's an example.

You want to start your own nail salon. You want to incorporate within your business model acrylic nails, manicures, pedicures, and nail health education. You also want to start providing massages. Remember we discussed diversification earlier. This is a wonderful way to diverse the portfolio of your business, by offering different services. Now, you don't have the startup capital needed to open your business at a thriving location. You don't have the startup capital needed to purchase all of the equipment needed. Does this mean that your business cannot actually operate? No.

What it does mean is that you have to start slowly until you have built that much needed capital. This is where your business plan comes into play.

Why not start by purchasing the items needed to do those acrylic nails, manicures and pedicures? A list of those items can range from nail files, emery boards, buffers, cuticle pushers, nail clippers, cotton balls, cutting pliers, portable hand/foot soakers, etc. Now, you've purchased your supplies, even if one at a time. Why not start advertising on Facebook and LinkedIn of these services? Well, you don't have a location yet; right? Why not start your business by actually GOING TO THE CUSTOMER? Many women (and men) would LOVE to have their nails done at home versus going to the actual salon. The advantages for the customer are: (1) NO WAIT; (2) NO WAIT; and (3) privacy. A lot of men would probably gravitate to this service. Not many men will even admit to ever getting manicures or pedicures. But isn't this a great way to still deliver great service AND build your clientele all at the same time.

Eventually, you would have built your client base. These clients will feel extremely confident in your services, will recommend you to others, and will then follow you anywhere, especially when you finally open that salon.

This is just an example which can be applied to any industry. Start SMALL especially when you don't have startup capital.

Always make sure that what you are offering is different and unique. This company is unique because the services are actually done at the client's home, versus an actual salon. This company is also unique because one of the services offered actually teaches the client about nail care, what should be done in between service appointments. This company is also unique because wait times are literally diminished, affording the client more time to attend to family and other personal avenues. Additionally, you can book your clients' next appointments IMMEDIATELY. Also, you can offer your clients the added advantage of having personal supplies just for them. For too often at these salons, you can't be guaranteed that the equipment has been sanitized. After all, filing boards are NOT sanitized; right? These are offerings you can give to your clients which will set you apart from any other nail salon in your area, or even in your state. Once again, these principles can be applied to almost any industry you're entering.

9

WRITE THE VISION

Are you even prepared for business ownership? Let's take this simple test. Who is the target market? How much will it take to operate your business monthly? Have you picked the right location? Where do you see your business within the next five years? What is the competition in your area? What need does your business serve? What problem does it solve?

> ***Habakkuk 2:2***
> *And the Lord answered me, and said, Write the vision, and make it plain upon tables, that he may run that readeth it.*

This is your business plan. Most people ONLY write a business plan when seeking funding from a bank or some other investor. While this is so true, you will need a business plan for these efforts to succeed, you should have a business plan regardless of whether or not you are seeking funding sources. A business plan just makes plain sense.

The vision you are writing ultimately becomes the business plan. A business plan is just that – a plan for your business. The only way your business will operate properly is if you have a plan for it. Your business plan allows you to see exactly what your business is and where you would like to see it mature into say in five years.

Why did you start this business? What is your industry? Do you know your target market? Why are you passionate about this particular industry? What need does your business solve? Is there a need for this type of business in your area? Who is your competition? Is there competition near your business location?

Why did you choose that particular location? How much are your startup expenses? Do you have employees? When will it be feasibly lucrative for the company to even hire employees? What startup equipment/supplies will you need? Have you researched your industry?

If you are not able to answer any of these questions, then you have not done your homework properly and are now ill-prepared for business ownership. It is totally YOUR responsibility to do the necessary research on your perspective industry. It is totally YOUR responsibility to know what sorts of bonding or insurances your industry demands. It is totally YOUR responsibility to know your competition. You must research your industry thoroughly to get a firm grasp on the pulse of your business.

Don't start your business off with laziness as your "modus operandi". I saw this quote once: "As you were deciding whether the glass was half empty or half full, I sold the glass." While you are taking your time focusing on things that don't matter, someone else is moving and shaking. While you are taking your PRECIOUS time focusing on things that don't matter, someone else has beat you to the punch. While you are taking your

VALUABLE time focusing on things that don't matter, someone else has started your business and has taken your customers. Laziness will get your nowhere.

Remember in the previous chapter where we discussed how important it is to change your mindset? Well, this is so true for that spirit of laziness, which I pray this day gets off you, in Jesus' Name. Laziness and Procrastination are essentially the same things; neither will get you where you want to go and neither will allow your dreams to become reality.

10

CONCLUSION

Let us come to the conclusion of the matter, fear God……

Anything worth having in life takes sacrifice, hard work, perseverance, endurance and passion. But most of all, it takes belief that God's Word is true and will certainly stand the test of time.

Business ownership is truly a remarkable accomplishment for anyone. Successful business ownership is the next logical step. If we take heed to follow these simple instructions, we are certain to prosper and have good SUCCESS. God's way is the ONLY WAY.

I pray that these words have entered your spirits with the humbleness and meekness solely intended.

I pray that you have been encouraged and motivated to move forward.

I pray that your questions have been answered and that those new businesses will begin with a zeal like never before.

I pray God's continued favor upon your lives and that He crowns all your efforts with much SUCCESS!!

Remember, God's plan for YOU is so much bigger than any plan you could possibly have for yourself.

To God be the glory for ALL THE GREAT THINGS He has done!!

About the Author

God placed within Shannon Barnes, a native of New Orleans, LA, an entrepreneur ministry at an early age. She finally brought that vision to fruition in 2008. Through all the trials and pitfalls, she was determined to help others achieve a level of not only SUCCESS, but of true excellence. It has been her sincere desire to see the people of God grow and mature in the things of God. She has extensive experience and expertise in motivational speaking, and hosting trainings, seminars, conferences, webinars, and workshops all aimed at preparing the entrepreneur for business ownership.

If you would like to book Mrs. Barnes to speak at your next event, please email her at: barnesgroup@outlook.com.

www.ingramcontent.com/pod-product-compliance
Lightning Source LLC
Chambersburg PA
CBHW070949180426
43194CB00041B/1994